100 tips

LADY OF THE LAKE PATTERN, Ann Hazelwood, St. Charles, Missouri.

American Quilter's Society

P. O. Box 3290 • Paducah, KY 42002-3290

www.AmericanQuilter.com

by
Ann Hazelwood from

AWARD-WINNING QUILTERS

Located in Paducah, Kentucky, the American Quilter's Society (AQS) is dedicated to promoting the accomplishments of today's quilters. Through its publications and events, AQS strives to honor today's quiltmakers and their work and to inspire future creativity and innovation in quiltmaking.

Text © 2008, Author, Ann Hazelwood
Artwork © 2008, American Quilter's Society
Executive Editor: Andi Reynolds
Senior Editor: Linda Baxter Lasco
Graphic Design: Marty Turner
Cover Design: Michael Buckingham
Photography: Charles R. Lynch, unless otherwise noted

American Quilter's Society
P. O. Box 3290 • Paducah, KY 42002-3290
www.AmericanQuilter.com

Additional copies of this book may be ordered from the American Quilter's Society, PO Box 3290, Paducah, KY 42002-3290, or online at www.AmericanQuilter.com.

Library of Congress Cataloging-in-Publication Data

Hazelwood, Ann Watkins.
  100 tips from award-winning quilters / by Ann Hazelwood.
    p. cm.
  ISBN 978-1-57432-964-3
  1. Patchwork. 2. Machine quilting. 3. Patchwork quilts. I. Title.
    II. Title: One hundred tips from award-winning quilters.

TT835.H358 2008
746.46--dc22

                                    2008030035

Proudly printed and bound in the
United States of America

Dedication

Any achievements in my life are due to supportive people I am fortunate to have around me:

Keith, my husband, who knows the value of time and the balance of work and pleasure.

My sons, Joel and Jason Watkins, who shake their heads in wonder, but smile with their approval.

My employees, who understand my interests on the other side of the counter.

Meredith Schroeder, one of my mentors in the quilt world, who gave us the American Quilter's Society, The National Quilt Museum, and this publishing opportunity.

Thank you all very much!

Collection of Meredith Schroeder, Paducah, Kentucky

Ann began her quilting career in 1970 with a home-based business. In 1979, she opened Patches etc. Quilt Shop in the historic district of St. Charles, Missouri. Two additional shops, Patches Craft Center and Patches Button Shoppe, soon followed.

Ann is a quilt historian, lecturer, and author of *Pretty Polka Dots* and the *Thought-a-Day Calendar for Today's Quilter*, as well as other quilt-related publications. In additon she has authored *100 Things to Do in St. Charles*, *100 Best Kept Secrets of Missouri*, and *100 Things You Need to Know If You Own a Quilt*.

A certified quilt appraiser with AQS who serves on the board of The National Quilt Museum in Paducah, Kentucky, Ann also curated an exhibit of her own quilt collection at the museum.

BRIDAL SHOWER QUILT, Ann Hazelwood, St. Charles, Missouri.

Contents

The contents of this book are meant to inspire, instruct and advise you. The tips are organized into sections: The Quilter as Student; Tools; Designing & Working Styles; Stash Savvy; Techniques; Quilting; Finishing Touches; and Show Etiquette. Scattered throughout you will find "Passion" pages, whose contributors speak to what moves and motivates all quilt makers to make award-winning quilts. Enjoy!

Collection of Meredith Schroeder, Paducah, Kentucky

Inspiration

Keep a written list of all the quilts you want to make. Use this list to help pick a topic or idea when it's time to start a new piece. Read about your subject, touch it, feel it, eat it, live with it, take pictures of it, talk about it, and do a Web search so you can understand every facet of it.

Be passionate about the subjects you choose for your quilts. Loving your image or idea will transform your work. You will become emotionally invested in it and do a much better job because of your commitment to the idea. The techniques and processes you use to construct the quilt will be more carefully chosen and executed.

Ann Fahl
www.annfahl.com
Racine, Wisconsin

Passion

Detail, Tea Party, Ann Fahl Racine, Wisconsin.

Detail, MEXICAN STAR, Nancy Page, St. Peter, Missouri.

The Quilter as Student

Learn All You Can

Use quilting and tools and techniques that work for YOU! Choose colors, fabrics, and patterns that excite YOU! Learn all you can about the techniques you are using and don't be afraid to try new colors and patterns that you have not tried before.

Nancy Page
nancyjpage@yahoo.com
St. Peter, Missouri

Know Your Machine

Get to know your sewing machine and what it is capable of doing for you. The more you know about it, the better the machine can work for you!

Purchase a single-hole throat plate for your machine. You will end up with straighter stitching.

Jean Biddick
www.jeanbiddick.com
Tucson, Arizona

Detail, Looking High and Low, Jean Biddick, Tucson, Arizona.

Hone Your Skills

Do the best job you can by honing your skills. Do this as you make the quilts that are most satisfying to YOU.

If you fall in love with your quilt and do your best (because after all the judges are looking for skill in execution), I think you are more likely to win! Your joy will show through in the visual impact and I think that is where a big part of a "win" begins.

Kathy Delaney
www.kathydelaney.com
Tucson, Arizona

Points

Technique counts! A little more time spent squaring corners or matching points can mean the difference between a mediocre quilt and a masterpiece.

Some art quilters seem to think that their quilts are exempt from traditional rules, but I don't agree. If an artist chooses to use a non-traditional technique, I'd like to think it's for a reason rather than because they don't have the skill to execute a technique well. If a quilt is worth making, it's worth doing well.

Cyndi Souder
www.moonlightingquilts.com
Annandale, Virginia

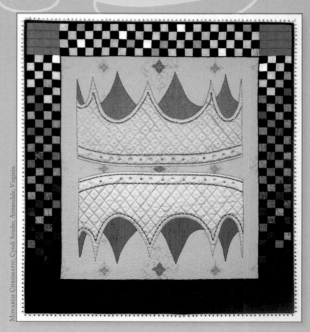

MONARCH CHROMATIC. Cyndi Souder, Annandale, Virginia.

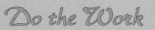

Do the Work

From the point of view of an abstract fiber artist, my best tip for anyone interested in art quilting is to do the work.

Learn the basic quilting techniques first, then do the work, do it more, and then some more! The more work you make, the better you get with composition, design, color, and expertise in putting it all together.

Don't worry about making a masterpiece. Just make art, and a lot of it!

Liz Berg
www.lizbergartquilts.com
Castro Valley, California

Detail Dance 3 Trepidation, Liz Berg Castro Valley California

Take a Novel Approach

I'm a self-taught quilter. My advice to others is to try a novel approach to a traditional idea. Stretch beyond working with others' patterns or copying other artists' work.

Phil Beaver
www.philbeaver.com
French Lick, Indiana

Detail, *Secrets of the Daylilies*, J. Phil Beaver, French Lick, Indiana.

Develop Your Own Style

Make quilts that showcase your unique talents and personality. If you excel at setting in seams, make quilts that emphasize that technique. If quilting is your forté, leave open spaces to highlight your quilting skill. If you love stripes, use them to accentuate your designs.

As you design quilts that feature your particular strengths, you'll begin to develop your own style. Making quilts of your own design that showcase your talents and reflect your personality is extremely satisfying, and often catches the judge's eye.

Sherri Bain Driver
sbdriver@mac.com
Tucson, Arizona

Detail Sonoran Stars, Sherri Bain Driver, Tucson, Arizona

It's Your Quilt

Before you take "tips" from others, remember that it is YOUR quilt! You do not have to follow anyone else's rules. You may use any combination of colors and embellishments as you see fit.

To me, art is what comes from the maker's inspiration. If your quilt wins a prize, GREAT! But it's the making that matters.

OUT OF THE STRONG CAME FORTH SWEETNESS, Zena Thorpe, Chatsworth, California. Inset: center detail of quilt.

Zena Thorpe
www.geocities.com/zenasquilts
Chatsworth, California

Detail, STRATA, Barbara J. Parady, Hamilton, Illinois.

Control Your Piece

Passion

Make art that you are compelled to make, not pieces designed to fit someone else's specific theme. Your artist's statement can show how your art fits the theme of a show. You'll be more satisfied as an artist if you control your piece rather than having some arbitrary theme controlling it!

Barbara Parady
www.bjparady.com
Hamilton, Illinois

Tools

Plastic

Just as Dustin Hoffman was told in "The Graduate," my tip is "plastic." I have probably every quilting ruler ever made, in every size, but there always seems to be a size or shape that I need and can't find commercially. So I head to the plastic store and seek out the ⅛" clear plastic.

I have the store cut it to the size I need and then I am ready to "square up" my block. I also have had plastic cut for templates that I use repeatedly. The heavier plastic allows me to rotary cut around the designs.

Clear plastic is also great if you need to match up motifs on your fabric. If you find you need to have some "semi-permanent" measurements on your clear plastic, use moveable neon ruler tape, available at most quilt shops.

Detail, It's Never Pointless, Mary Kay Davis, Sunnyvale, California.

Mary Kay Davis
http://mkdthreads.com
Sunnyvale, California

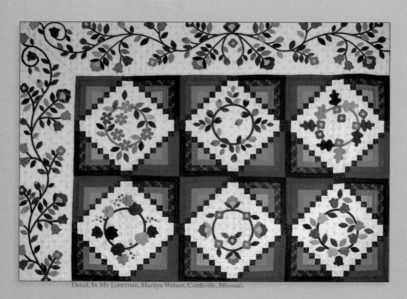

Detail, IN MY LIFETIME, Marilyn Webert, Cottleville, Missouri.

Marking

When marking a quilt for quilting, always test the method on a scrap of the fabric you are using to ensure it can be removed if needed.

Marilyn Webert
mkwilts@hotmail.com
Cottleville, Missouri

Back Story

I was once unable to remove the markings
from a quilt. Not wanting to give up on my
creation, I made the front of my whole-
cloth quilt the back. The quilt was
placed in several shows, and won
a total of three ribbons before
I sold it. So you can judge the
back of the quilt as its cover!

Marilyn Robinson
mrobinson02@netscape.net
St. Peters, Missouri

Detail, MAGICAL MEDALLIONS, Karen Kay Buckley, Carlisle, Pennsylvania. Background rectangle added.

Make Perfect Circles

For both hand- and machine-appliquéd circle shapes, I developed a product based on the great results I was getting with my method of making circles. I call it "Perfect Circles" because every time I got an evaluation back from the judges on my quilts, they always wrote "perfect circles."

Karen Kay Buckley
www.karenkaybuckley.com
Carlisle, Pennsylvania

Keep It Neat

To tame wound bobbins, use ½" diameter vinyl tubing that is available at any hardware store. Slice the tubing into circles the width of your bobbins and cut it open on one side. The vinyl will wrap neatly around the thread.

Libby Lehman
www.libbylehman.us
Houston, Texas

Denali, Detavor, Libby Lehman, Houston, Texas.

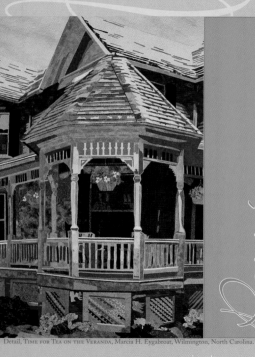

Refuse to Compromise

The most important thing to achieving success is to be true to yourself. Over the years, people have advised me to simplify my process so I could create more quilts per year. I have chosen to make incredibly intricate quilts that take months to create. The quilts that have won awards are always the pieces that I refused to compromise on, whether it was the size or intricacy or colors used.

I let the quilt tell me how large it needs to be or how intricate the appliqué. Most importantly, all processes are executed with extreme care so that the quilt is the best work I can create.

Marcia H. Eygabroat
www.quiltedartworks.com
Wilmington, North Carolina

Passion

Detail, TIME FOR TEA ON THE VERANDA, Marcia H. Eygabroat, Wilmington, North Carolina.

Designing & Working Styles

Ideas Galore

Detail, Garden Maze, Irma Gail Hatcher, Conway, Arkansas

Courtesy of The National Quilt Museum, Paducah, Kentucky.

Irma Gail Hatcher
www.irmagailhatcher.com
Conway, Arkansas

When I begin working on a quilt, I have many ideas running through my head. Should I include this or that in the basic structure? I try not to think "that would be too much work" or "that would be too hard." If the idea would make the quilt better, then I go ahead and include it. Those little ideas that take a long time and a lot of effort are the very things that make a masterpiece.

Always use your best workmanship because every quilt is a self-portrait of the person who made it. Autograph your work with excellence.

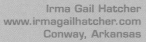

Prizewinning Quilts

As an NQA Certified Quilt Judge, I am asked for advice on making a "prizewinning quilt." My answer is two-fold:

- Pay attention to detail. As you are working on your composition, ask yourself, "What can I do to make this quilt better?"

- Simpler techniques or designs done exceedingly well rate higher than more complex designs or techniques poorly executed.

Carol Butzke
www.quiltappraisers.org/butzke.htm
Slinger, Wisconsin

Background rectangles added.

BRIGHT HOPES, BRIGHT PROMISE,　　　　Carol Butzke, Slinger, Wisconsin.

Break It Down

When working on a large project it helps to "break it down" into little bits. It makes it less intimidating and keeps me focused.

While designing, I break off a section and draw the details out. This enables me to visualize which fabrics are working well together and also lets me start sewing, which I enjoy most!

When I am working from a photograph and making fabric choices, I use "sticky notes" or index cards to block off the rest of the photo. I don't think about the whole project, just the section I am working on.

Cynthia England
www.englanddesign.com
Dickinson, Texas

Detail, OPEN SEASON, Cynthia England, Dickinson, Texas.

Drafting

It takes pencil and paper to turn an idea into a pattern, with many revisions along the way. I have many ideas sketched onto graph paper and revisit my stack from time to time to look at each emerging pattern with fresh eyes and incorporate new ideas. When it is time to start a new project, there always seems to be a particular design that fits the fabrics I want to work with.

The last step with every quilt is to make a final drawing of what was done, including notations as to threads, fabrics, stitching patterns, and quilting designs used. You can't see where you are going unless you can look at where you have been.

Marla K. Yeager
www.cherrywoodfabrics.com
Ava, Missouri

Courtesy of The National Quilt Museum, Paducah, Kentucky.

Detail, BUCKSKIN, Marla K. Yeager, Ava, Missouri.

Visualizing by Planning

I make a plan and use all the tools I have at my disposal to visualize the details. I use image editing software such as Adobe Photoshop as a visual aid. By manipulating my own ideas, changing colors and shapes, layering, and trying out backgrounds, I can see what will work. I explore all the "What ifs" without wasting yardage.

I find I work better when I go though this process and create some sort of guide. But I also let myself be free to change and let serendipity happen along the way.

Michelle Verbeeck
www.michelleverbeeck.com
Dover, Pennsylvania

Essence, Michelle Verbeeck, Dover, Pennsylvania.

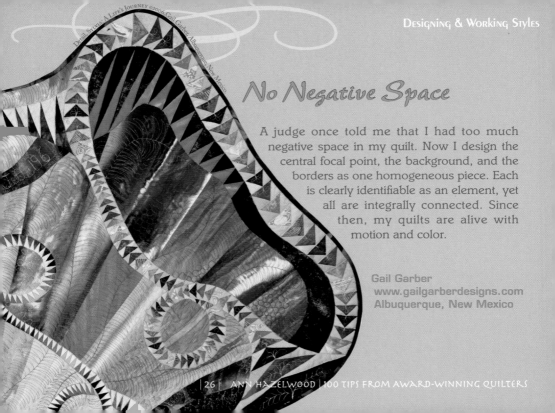

No Negative Space

A judge once told me that I had too much negative space in my quilt. Now I design the central focal point, the background, and the borders as one homogeneous piece. Each is clearly identifiable as an element, yet all are integrally connected. Since then, my quilts are alive with motion and color.

Gail Garber
www.gailgarberdesigns.com
Albuquerque, New Mexico

Be Visual

Make your visual decisions visually! When you are faced with a design decision while working on a quilt, don't wonder what you should do. Try out your options visually by holding up fabric to your quilt on the design wall, sketching or doing fabric mock-ups on paper, or even doing computer sketching.

Getting ideas in front of your eyes will lead to an easier decision than trying to imagine the solution in your head.

Lorraine Torrence
www.lorrainetorrence.com
Seattle, Washington

Detail, THUNDERCLOUDS APPROACHING, Lorraine Torrence, Seattle, Washington

Detail, I Must Be Hexed, Cheryl See, Ashburn, Virginia.

Let Your Quilt Speak

Some of my quilts did not go in the direction I originally thought they were headed. Quilts have a mind of their own and if you have an open mind you can hear them speak to you.

Keep an open mind. Whatever your inspiration, whether it be a fabric, technique, or design, it could give you inspiration for the rest of the quilt. Often it will be colors that you never thought you would put together, but somehow they work.

Cheryl See
cseequilter@comcast.net
Ashburn, Virginia

Listen with Your Eyes

I try to "listen with my eyes." If I am uncomfortable with a fabric or color choice for any reason, I pull it out and try more fabrics and colors. It can make for a pile of discards, but when the final outcome looks right, both close up and far away, the clean up is worth it.

Sheila Steers
ststeers@comcast.net
Eugene, Oregon

In the Morning Calm, Sheila Steers, Eugene, Oregon.

Use a Work Wall

ROOFTOP ANGLES, Jane Blair, Wyomissing, Pennsylvania. Background rectangle added.

Never take fabric for granted. A design relies on the choice of fabric to be successful.

From your working sketch, make two full-size drawings of the whole quilt. Place one on the work wall and cut apart the second for templates. Using these templates, audition fabric on the wall for each piece until the entire quilt looks satisfactory and pleasing.

Fabrics take on a different look next to other fabrics. With this method you can stand back and see what works with what.

Jane Blair
www.janeblairquilts.com
Wyomissing, Pennsylvania

Spice up a traditional quilt by incorporating a variety of techniques. Combine paper foundation piecing with hand
appliqué. Add embroidery and reverse appliqué. Mix
hand and machine quilting. Insert double piping
next to a pieced border.

I used all of these techniques in
my PHANTASY quilt.

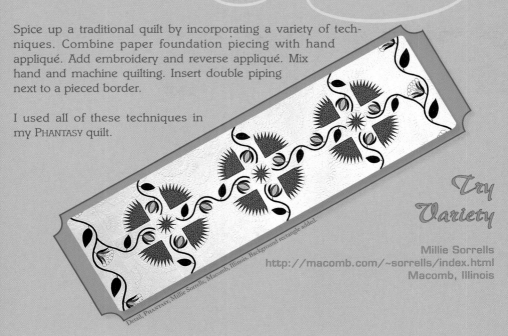

Detail, PHANTASY, Millie Sorrells, Macomb, Illinois. Background rectangle added.

Try
Variety

Millie Sorrells
http://macomb.com/~sorrells/index.html
Macomb, Illinois

Simplicity

The Secret Garden in a Starry, Starry Night, Rami Kim, Granite Bay, California.

My passion is designing exciting and stylish wearable art that creates a visual impact without eclipsing the wearer. Each facet of the design must have its own place of importance while still interacting harmoniously with all the other elements.

As pedestrian as it sounds, the quintessence of my design success is simplicity. It's practicing artistic restraint while keeping my eye on the grace of the style. Having the discipline to limit myself to a balance of colors and techniques is not always easy, but the reward is always elegance.

Rami Kim
www.ramikim.com
Granite Bay, California

Background First

When I make wall quilts for my dimensional flowers, I always make my complete background first, including the borders, binding, and machine quilting. Then I make the flowers and audition them on the quilt background.

When I am satisfied with the design, I stitch the flowers in place. On some quilts, I attach them with Velcro® tape so I can change the flowers with the seasons and holidays.

Barb Broshous
www.2bara.com
Colorado Springs, Colorado

Detail, Daffodils And Crocus, Barb Broshous, Colorado Springs, Colorado.

Listen While You Work

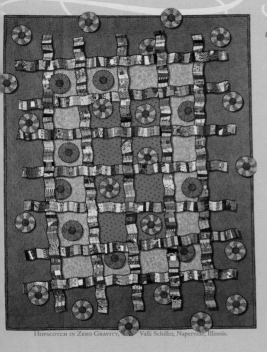

Hopscotch in Zero Gravity, by Valli Schiller, Naperville, Illinois.

It's often the extra intricate details (zillions of teeny pieces, embellishments, intensive quilting, unique edge treatments) that take a quilt from "great" to "award winning." These details can take a lot of tedious time to execute.

I love listening to audio books while I work on mindless, repetitive tasks. The stories engage my mind and keep me interested while I am plugging away. When I'm asked how long it took me to quilt that, my answer is usually something like "two volumes of Harry Potter on tape."

I keep my CD player on the opposite side of the room so that I am forced to get up and walk across the room to change discs. Stretching and mini-breaks help me avoid overwork injuries.

Valli Schiller
vschiller@wideopenwest.com
Naperville, Illinois

Be Passionate!

My art quilts evolve from my heart. I love fabric. I love color. I love to stitch. This evokes my passion to create.

Passion
- drives my desire to experiment,
- energizes me to convey a story or message,
- propels me to be persistent,
- stimulates a little playfulness and serendipity as I work,
- pushes me to do the best that I can, and
- challenges me to finish!

Your passion can do the same for you.

Wendy Butler Berns
www.wendybutlerberns.com
Lake Mills, Wisconsin

Detail, W.B.B.-WENDELLA B. BUTTERFLY, Wendy Butler Berns, Lake Mills, Wisconsin.

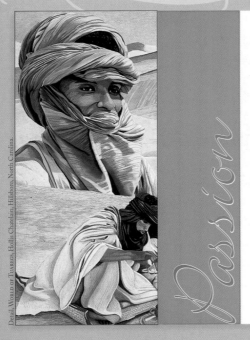

Detail, WORLD OF TUAREGS, Hollis Chatelain, Hillsboro, North Carolina.

Passion

The Love of Quilting

Keep quilting sacred by not compromising. Since we have so many things that we are required to do, do only what you love to do in your quilting.

If you enjoy making quilts for others, then make them with the patterns and colors that you love. If you love to sell quilts, then create ones that make your heart sing, not what everyone thinks will sell. If you love to make tops, then have someone quilt them for you. If you love to hand quilt, please don't feel you need to start machine quilting because everyone else is.

Find out what you love and do it! This way your quilts will be a gift to the world and a gift to you!

Hollis Chatelain
www.hollisart.com
Hillsboro, North Carolina

Use Your Stash

I go to my own stash first, every time I start a new project. My theory is that my stash contains the fabrics that I liked most at all the quilt shops I've visited. Therefore, my favorite fabrics are at home and that is the best place to start.

An easy way to pick fabrics for a quilt is to find a fabric that you really like and use it as your color palette to guide fabric selection, then save that original fabric for the borders.

Cindy Squyres
squyres@charter.net
Martin, Tennessee

Detail, WOODLAND CREATURES, Cindy Squyres, Martin, Tennessee. Background rectangle added.

Same Color, Different Fabrics

TRUMPET LILIES, Debra Danko, Grand Blanc, Michigan.

Don't be stuck on using the same fabrics repeatedly in your project. Instead, try to use different fabrics within the same color family. In my TRUMPET LILIES quilt that was on the cover of the 2005 AQS Wall Calendar, all the petals are orange, but I used many different fabrics.

Mixing in fabrics with slight variations in print, pattern, tone, value, or texture enhances the quilt. If I had repeatedly used the same fabric for every petal, the result would have been flat and lifeless.

Debra Danko
www.debradanko.com
Grand Blanc, Michigan

Mix It Up

Don't be afraid to use nontraditional fabrics in unconventional ways. I work almost exclusively with vintage fabrics and love to mix blocks and fabrics of different eras with new fabric purchases.

Go ahead and add that scrap of linen that makes your heart sing or reminds you of a treasured memory. The "quilt police" may frown but I have chosen to ignore their voices and follow my heart instead.

Mary Kerr
www.marywkerr.com
Woodbridge, Virginia

Detail, Orange You Glad You're Mine.

Mary Kerr, Woodbridge, Virginia. Background rectangle added.

Detail, Kaleidoscopic XXX: Cosmic Carp, Paula Nadlestern, The Bronx, New York. Background circle added.

No Solids

For the record, I never use solid color fabrics. I choose and collect fabrics that "read like a solid." They are crammed with lots of shadings and tone-on-tone effects. They are a source of luminosity and dimension.

A finished quilt that seems dimensional is always more interesting to me than one that reads as virtually "flat."

Paula Nadlestern
www.paulanadelstern.com
The Bronx, New York

Using Prints

I make animal quilts and I love using prints to add texture and interest to my portraits. Surprisingly, you do not need to limit yourself to fabrics that look exactly like fur, feathers, scales, skin, etc., as long as you have the shape and the color of the animal and you add some contrast (lights and darks).

You can use a wide variety of prints that merely suggest what you are trying to portray, such as stripes for long fur, along with unexpected bits of checks or florals.

Try adding some prints that you normally wouldn't use and see what happens. Hopefully you will start to look at fabric in a whole new way and begin to see a new world of possibilities.

Nancy S. Brown
http://members.aol.com/nancybrownquilts
Oakland, California

WANTED, Nancy S. Brown, Oakland, California. Inset, quilt square detail.

Twilight Dance, Charla Gee, Littleton, Colorado.

Be Brave with Color

The right combination of color and contrast can add depth and dimension to an otherwise ordinary quilt. There are such incredible fabrics available right now; use them, love them, and create with them. Trust your instincts — YOU are the artist!

Charla Gee
geec13@comcast.net
Littleton, Colorado

Fabric Values

Color seems to get all the credit in a quilt, but value does all the work, so pay attention to your choice of value before color. Many of us are not drawn to those lighter value fabrics, but if you don't include some in your quilt, you will get less depth in your design.

Remember to make visual decisions visually, not intellectually. Many quilters try to decide on color or design by talking about what they want to do, instead of just trying it. The only way to really decide if a design or color plan is going to work is to lay it out and look at it. It should then become obvious.

Carol Taylor
www.caroltaylorquilts.com
Pittsford, New York

Detail, Dispersion, Carol Taylor, Pittsford, New York

Other Fabric Sources

Not all wonderful fabric comes on a bolt! I've used everything from a bottle green cotton lace tablecloth to Crown Royal® whisky bags on a quilt.

Some of my finest fabrics come from thrift shop clothing. Check the labels, not only for the fiber content, but also to judge condition. A fresh tag means a lightly used garment. Launder the item, remove all seams and buttons, and fold flat so it is ready to use. Your stash will expand just for pennies, and you'll find it much easier to cut into those fabrics that are beautiful but not so financially dear.

Detail, CHURCH LADIES, Teddy Pruett, Lake City, Florida. Background rectangle added.

Teddy Pruett
www.teddypruett.com
Lake City, Florida

Save Your Bias

I keep different colors, designs, and patterns of bias strips from previous projects in a box. They come in handy when you need a colorful vine or stem. When the creative urge hits, no need to stop and cut bias, just use what you have.

For stems, fold bias strips in half, wrong sides together, lengthwise; pin in place, and sew close to the fold either by hand or machine. Trim close to the stitching, press over to cover the stitching, and appliqué.

Karen Burns
kmburns@surewest.net
Granite Bay, California

Detail, IN THE HEART OF THE GARDEN, Karen Burns, Granite Bay, California. Background rectangle added.

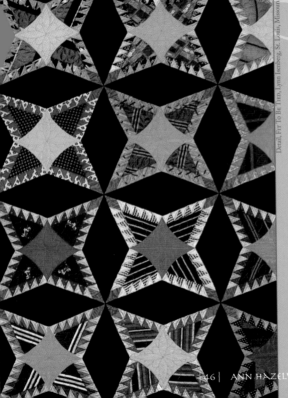

Detail, Fer To Be Tien, Lynn Isenberg, St. Louis, Missouri.

Scrap Quilts

When making a "scrap quilt," try to think of each block in the quilt as an individual mini-quilt. When the blocks come together in the quilt, they seem married.

When not working with blocks, be brave and daring in your fabric choices. Several "uglies" will become beautiful as a small part of the whole quilt. The combination of fabrics makes it more interesting to the viewer and more fun for you to make.

Lynn Isenberg
(no e-mail)
St. Louis, Missouri

Detail, AFTER THE RAIN, Mary L. Hackett, Carbondale, Illinois.

Set Your Own Standards

Passion

The most successful quilts I have made are those that I felt passionate about making. Something about the idea, inspiration, or technique (or all three) fired me up to the point that I could not resist making the piece.

I don't need the "quilt police." I have my own standards and they're often higher than anyone else could know. I am incapable of doing less than my personal best.

Mary L. Hackett
www.marylhackett.com
Carbondale, Illinois

Playing with Shapes

Detail, GROUND COVER I, Jane Sassaman, Harvard, Illinois.

Jane Sassaman
www.janesassaman.com
Harvard, Illinois

I use a lot of independent shapes to create my collaged compositions. If the pieces are small enough, I like to work on the table instead of the wall, so gravity can hold the shapes down and my composing will be more spontaneous, just like "quilting on a ouija board."

I begin with a solid colored background fabric and build the design on it. Occasionally I'll have everything placed nicely and begin to wonder if a different background fabric would be better. I'll slip a piece of Plexiglas under my shapes so I can lift the whole composition without the background. Since it is clear, I can audition other choices with minimal disturbance to the placement of the pieces.

Creating Machine Appliqué on Tulle

For appliqués with many pieces, I draw or copy the appliqué design on paper, trace the design onto freezer paper, and number each piece on both the original and freezer-paper. I cut a piece of tulle, place it over the original, secure it with a dab of glue stick, and use it as a base for reassembling the appliqué.

Back each piece of fabric to be used with double-sided iron-on adhesive, use the freezer-paper templates to cut out the pieces, and reassemble the motifs, placing each numbered piece on the tulle over its corresponding number. Lift the tulle with the completed design and place it on your quilt. Using a pressing cloth, fuse the appliqué, stitch to secure, and cut away the excess tulle after the outer edges are finished.

Yolanda Ann Reardon
ann reardon@huges.net
Eggleston, Virginia

Detail, Tree of Life, Yolanda Ann Reardon, Eggleston, Virginia.

Keeping Grainline Straight

When doing appliqué, I use freezer paper to trace the pattern and mark the straight-of-grain lines right on the freezer paper. Then I cut out the pattern and iron the freezer-paper pieces on the right side of the fabrics, matching the grainlines. Then I trace around the freezer-paper piece.

This technique keeps the pattern in place, makes an accurate piece, and keeps the grainlines straight.

Nancy Hahn
nhan1@charter.net
St. Peters, Missouri

Detail, THANKS SUZANNE! Nancy Hahn, St. Peters, Missouri.

Chain Piecing

When chain piecing, keep precut pieces for a different project near your machine. At the end of the chain, instead of putting a scrap of fabric through the machine to keep the threads engaged, sew a pair of pieces from the precut group. This keeps threads from pulling into the machine and getting tangled up as well as creating a set of blocks.

This is how I made my MINI 9-PATCH. As I worked on other projects, I kept the 1" squares by my machine. It took nine years to sew the almost 15,000 pieces together and another 67 hours to quilt it on my home sewing machine.

Lois Jarvis
www.loisjarvisquilts.com
Madison, Wisconsin

My Mini 9-Patch, Lois Jarvis, Madison, Wisconsin.

Background squares added.

Pressing Machine-Pieced Quilts

Starching yardage prior to cutting your patches will help keep quilt blocks from becoming distorted when they are pressed later during construction.

Pass a hot iron over the wrong side of your fabric before spraying starch. The starch will immediately sink into the warm fabric. Use a dry iron, not a steam iron, so moisture won't sit in the iron to later be spit out as brownish spots on your fabric.

Anita Grossman Solomon
www.makeitsimpler.com
New York, New York

Detail, KEY WEST BEAUTY, Anita Grossman Solomon, New York, New York. Multiple images used.

Piecing Miniatures

When piecing miniatures, most books will suggest that you sew a ⅛" seam allowance. I have found that it works much better to use a larger seam allowance so that there is something to hang onto while you are working.

I sew a ½" seam allowance and then clip it to about ⅛" after pressing.

Janet S. Dove
(no e-mail)
McPherson, Kansas

Detail, Miniature Lone Star, Janet S. Dove, McPherson, Kansas

Sewing Miniature Blocks Together

When joining blocks together, I do not use pins to hold them. My blocks will have up to 60 or 70 pieces and are quite thick. When I try to pin them together, they have a tendency to shift, making it very hard to keep them aligned.

To keep the blocks aligned, I use double-faced tape while joining them. I place the tape outside the seam line, being careful not to sew through the tape. The best part of this method is that you can slightly open the blocks before sewing to be sure they are lined up properly. If not, they can easily be shifted into alignment.

George Siciliano
www.georgesiciliano.com
Lebanon, Pennsylvania

Detail, SAMARKAND, George Siciliano, Lebanon, Pennsylvania. Multiple images used.

Crazy Quilt Foundation Piecing

I usually like to precut all my pieces when doing a Crazy Quilt block. Because the shapes are so irregular, I like to use my computer program on this step. I set up the block (original drawing), then print out the pattern with a second mirror image copy of the block.

By cutting up one copy, I can use the pattern pieces as templates to cut out my chosen fabrics, leaving about ½" extra fabric on all sides. This helps tremendously with placement of each fabric piece on the muslin background of the block.

Betty Lenz
www.bettylenzquilts.com
Marshall, Missouri

Nearly Nouveau, Betty Lenz, Marshall, Missouri.

Paper Foundation Piecing

If you make a mistake doing foundation paper piecing and need to remove the last piece after you've already trimmed the seam allowance, try this. Put transparent tape on the back side of the foundation paper, grab the fabric, and tear the offending seam off the paper. This will leave your paper intact while you pick out the seam. You can then sew another piece on correctly without having to redo your paper template.

Use freezer paper with a small stitch length so it will tear off easily when you're done.

Ricky Tims
www.rickytims.com
La Veta, Colorado

Simple Gifts, Ricky Tims, La Veta, Colorado.

No Shadowing

Judges frown on "shadowing," which occurs when a light fabric meets a dark fabric and the darker seam allowance is visible through the lighter fabric.

When foundation piecing, you can't always iron the seam towards the dark fabric. Solution: tint fabric paint close to your light color. On the back side of the fabric, smear the paint on with a sponge, covering the darker edge completely. Heat-set with a hot iron on cotton setting and — voilá — no more shadows. Your light fabric will glow against the dark.

Jill Bryant
www.quilterjill.com
Chesterfield, Missouri

KALEIDOSCOPE, Jill Bryant, Chesterfield, Missouri.

Natural Effects

When making pictorial or landscape quilts that need a natural effect, such as foliage, I want the edges to be a little rough looking, not smooth. I use raw-edge appliqué, which can be fused or not. The key is in stitching the edges.

Use a straight stitch and criss-cross the edges, sewing in a somewhat random pattern to turn smooth edges into leafy ones. The stitching secures the edges to reduce fraying while obscuring the smooth cut edge and creating a natural looking variability in the foliage.

Detail, WILMINGTON TURRET,

Detail, LEXINGTON OFF MAIN, Susan

Sue Brittingham
sbrih@swva.net
Riner, Virginia

Brittingham, Riner, Virginia. Background rectangle added.

Beading

Not every quilt is a candidate for bead embellishment, but when appropriate, beads can enhance an area of a quilt to catch the viewer's attention. The eye is drawn to the sparkle, which invites further inspection.

Be sure the embellished areas deserve the extra scrutiny.

Breeze, Rachel Wetzler, St. Charles, Illinois. Courtesy of The National Quilt Museum, Paducah, Kentucky.

Rachel Wetzler
rachelwetzler@yahoo.com
St. Charles, Illinois

Beading Quilts

To maintain proper thread tension when beading, secure the base fabric in a hoop or a PVC frame. I recommend using NYMO® beading thread to attach the beads.

Mary Stori
www.marystori.com
Clyde, North Carolina

Detail, RAINFOREST ROYALTY, Mary Stori, Clyde, North Carolina.

Background squares added.

Photo Transfers

When making photo transfers to cloth, experiment with images of everyday objects. For a travel-themed quilt, scan travel documents, foreign currency, museum stubs, souvenir brochures, etc. Print them out onto photo-transfer fabric. Cut out the images and apply the objects one by one to your quilt, along with your transferred photographs.

I've successfully scanned and added three-dimensional objects to my quilts such as plates, silverware, jewelry, leaves, pressed flowers, and fishing reels. When in doubt, see how the object looks scanned and go from there. I think you will be surprised!

Ann Bodle-Nash
annbodlenash.wetpaint.com
Bow, Washington

Detail, NATURE.....IN LIVING COLOUR, Ann Bodle-Nash, Bow, Washington.

Detail, And Dragons, Too..., Suzanne Marshall, St. Louis, Missouri.

Add Embroidery

Add an embroidered outline to appliqué to enhance and define it. Using embroidery floss and an out-lilne stitch, sew through the background right next to the appliqué shapes. Do this after the appliqué is finished and before the quilt batting and backing are added. The embroidery will separate the appliqué from the background, adding accent and depth.

Suzanne Marshall
www.suzannequilts.com
St. Louis, Missouri

Practice, Practice, Practice

My advice to machine quilters is "practice, practice, practice." That, along with a good sewing machine, is the secret to improving your machine quilting.

I think people are very hard on themselves over their first efforts at quilting. Most of us will not make an award-winning quilt right away. For me the journey is all about progress, not perfection. As long as I am having fun, it is a worthwhile, creative pursuit.

Anne Lullie
annelullie@gmail.com
Lake in the Hills, Illinois

COLORPLAY III, Anne Lullie, Lake in the Hills, Illinois.

Detail, Unexpected Beauty, Sandra Leichner, Albany, Oregon. Courtesy of The National Quilt Museum, Paducah, Kentucky.

Correct or Camouflage

A machine-quilting technique can be one of the best ways to correct or camouflage those not-so-perfect edges that occur as you are developing your hand-appliqué skills.

Machine quilt tightly on the background as close as possible to the outside edge of the appliqué shape, without encroaching onto the appliqué. The edges will magically curl under just a tad more from the "fill" of the batting and will look much smoother. Do this as you are quilting the background or after all other quilting has been completed, using invisible thread.

Sandra Leichner
http://home.comcast.net/~angelperch
Albany, Oregon

Quilting Design

The quilting designs you choose for your quilt should be as much of a priority in planning your quilt as the quilt top itself. I plan the quilting designs long before the other techniques. I can always decrease or increase the pattern later.

Mark the inside areas of your blocks before they are pieced. By planning backwards, the hard part is over and you can be enthusiastic about the finish line.

Sharon Schamber
www.sharonschamber.com
Payson, Arizona

Detail, THE FLOWER OF LIFE, Sharon Schamber, Payson, Arizona. Courtesy of The National Quilt Museum, Paducah, Ky.

Detail, A Visit to Provence, Diane Gaudynski, Pewaukee, Wisconsin.

Courtesy of The National Quilt Museum, Paducah, Kentucky.

Machine Quilting

Just because a quilting design is designated "continuous line" doesn't mean you can't stop while quilting it. The "zone" under the needle in a home sewing machine isn't very big, and it is often necessary to quilt part of the design, stop the machine, take a breath, and readjust the quilt and your hands before proceeding.

To avoid getting awkward stitches as you start again, raise the needle to the "up" position, make sure the quilt is exactly where you want it, then slowly resume your quilting. You'll get a smooth, even design with no glaring points where you had to stop.

Diane Gaudynski
www.dianegaudynski.net
Pewaukee, Wisconsin

Starting and Stopping

I start and stop often while I'm quilting, either to change thread colors or to move to a different area. Before starting, pull the bobbin thread to the top of the quilt by tugging on the top thread after the needle has pierced the quilt just once. Take a series of tiny stitches in the first ¼" of the quilting line to secure the threads. Trim both threads close to the surface, being careful not to cut the quilt.

End in the same way, with several tiny stitches, then take one more normal-length stitch to allow enough slack for pulling the bobbin thread to the top. Lift the presser foot and move the quilt from under the needle. Pull on the top thread and the bobbin thread will easily pop to the top. Cut both threads close to the surface. With this method, your threads are secure and you never have to burrow under your quilt to trim the threads.

FEATHER FLOWER #1, Caryl Bryer Fallert, Paducah, Kentucky.

Caryl Bryer Fallert
www.bryerpatch.com
Paducah, Kentucky

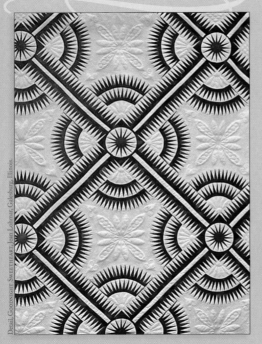

Detail, Goodnight Sweethearts, Jean Lohmar, Galesburg, Illinois.

Watch Where You're Going!

When you are machine quilting and you stop with the needle down for taking a breath or repositioning your hands, be ready to move the fabric as the needle comes up and you begin to stitch. If you don't get the move on, you will see a slub of thread on the back side. This usually happens when using the heavier decorative threads on the top. Fine silk thread and #60 needles are more forgiving.

Anticipation is the name of the game. Watch where you are going, not where you are! Like driving your car, anticipate the speed and curves ahead.

Jean Lohmar
www.heirloomsoftomorrow.net
Galesburg, Illinois

Quilting Patterns

For me the machine quilting is an integral part of the design process, not just an afterthought. I envision what I want the finished quilting to look like and then design the quilting to fit that image.

When I first began quilting, I had no clue as to how to "quilt as desired." Often the fabric I had chosen was such a busy print that the quilting was virtually invisible. Borders and blocks were always the wrong size to make use of the stencils I had.

Now while working on a project, fabrics are chosen to best highlight the quilting stitches and the size of the blocks and borders are determined by the quilting motifs and designs I want to use.

Elizabeth Spannring
http://elizabethspannring.com
La Center, Washington

Denali Sunflowers, Elizabeth Spannring, La Center, Washington

When Is Enough Quilting Enough?

Karen McTavish quilt image reprinted with permission from On-Word Bound Books. SILVER THREADS by Karen McTavish from **Whitework Quilting** by On-Word Bound Books, 2004. Photo by Steve Tiggman of Jeff Frey and Associates. Detail, SILVER THREADS, Karen McTavish, Duluth, Minnesota. Background square added.

I have the secret to machine quilting show-quality quilts.

I try to design unique and original quilting motifs for the quilt, then follow my set of rules to finish the quilt:

- Do what a hand quilter would do.
- Do the hardest thing.
- Never take a shortcut.

Karen McTavish
www.designerquilts.com
Duluth, Minnesota

Thread Colors

Many of my quilts are created from original photographs, printed on cloth, then enhanced with free-motion stitching. For some areas of the quilt, I choose thread colors that are close to the colors in the image. To highlight or accentuate an area, I select a thread that is a darker or lighter shade than the printed image. To achieve a sense of realism, one color thread is often less effective than using several different shades of one tone.

To draw the viewer's eye to a specific area of the composition, I will highlight it with a bit of contrasting color or by outlining it with a darker thread.

Carol Watkins
www.carolwatkins.com
Boulder, Colorado

Detail, Earth Poem, Carol Watkins, Boulder, Colorado. Background rectangle added.

Ending Threads

When ending a quilting line of heavier threads, it is easy to pull on the bobbin thread to get both threads onto the back side of your project to tie a knot. The starting end of your stitch line is a bit of a challenge because both ends are on the top of your quilt. Get around this by making a single stitch (up and down once) about an inch away from the start of your quilting line, then sew as usual. When you're done, just turn the project over and grab the inch long "handle" of thread that's waiting to let you pull both beginning threads to the back for knotting.

Melody Crust
www.melodycrust.com
Kent, Washington

Detail, XISHUANGBANNA (SHEE-SHANG-BANNA), Melody Crust, Kent, Washington.

Animal Quilts

When making pictorial quilts of animals, quilting details will give a more lifelike and pleasing appearance to the portrait. Using a dark thread, quilt a small circle around the pupil of the eye. Then, using a light color thread, quilt a small crescent just outside of the dark circle. You can also add a small dot by stitching in place near the upper side of the eye.

The dark stitching will cause the center of the eye to dome out slightly so it appears to be round and the light stitching will provide lifelike highlights.

Sharon Malec
www.malec-designs.com
West Chicago, Illinois

Quilting Straight Lines

When hand quilting straight lines, I always use ¼" masking tape. I purchase the tape at an auto parts store and get the largest roll I can find. I lay the tape on the quilt and stitch as close as possible to the tape without touching it. Do not stitch on the other side of the tape or you will get a wavy line.

Once I've finished the line, I remove the tape and throw it away. The masking tape will not leave a residue and there are no marked lines to remove.

Virginia Siciliano
www.georgesiciliano.com
Lebanon, Pennsylvania

Detail, Soil Festivities, Virginia Siciliano, Lebanon, Pennsylvania.

Hand Quilting

When hand quilting, change your needles often. A sharp needle will go through all layers of fabric and batting with ease. Your needle will become dull with repeated use. It does not make any difference if you purchase expensive or inexpensive needles.

I use size 8 or 9 betweens needles and switch to a new needle every 20 to 30 hours of quilting. On an average large hand-quilted quilt, I use around 18 needles.

Always dispose of your old needles by wrapping them in tape before throwing them away.

Charlotte Huber
(no e-mail)
Ferguson, Missouri

Detail, Missouri Waltz, Charlotte Huber, Ferguson, Missouri. Multiple images used.

WELCOME TO MY DREAMS, Betty Ekern Suiter, Racine, Wisconsin.

Batting and Quilting

To protect the batting while you are hand quilting, cut the backing at least 4" larger than the top. After the quilt is basted, fold the backing over the top and baste along the edges. The batting will be protected and will always come to the edge of the finished quilt.

Betty Ekern Suiter
www.bettyekernsuiter.com
Racine, Wisconsin

Quilting a Miniature

I hand quilt with a stab-stitch method for
my minis to keep the stitch size in proportion to the pattern. I often have machine
and hand quilting on the same quilt.
I like to mark with a blue wash-
out pen or the Clover® white
pen that can be removed by
water or ironing.

I square up and cut my quilt before I
add the binding, which I cut 1⅛" wide.
There's no need to use double-fold binding
on a miniature.

Connie Chunn
conniesminis@hotmail.com
Webster Groves, Missouri

Detail, Starring the Ladies, Connie Chunn, Webster Groves, Missouri.

Detail, Spice of Life, Linda M. Roy, Knoxville, Tennessee. Courtesy of The National Quilt Museum, Paducah, Kentucky

Crosshatching

I have developed a style that consists primarily of original appliqué. Something I frequently do to support my designs is to incorporate scale changes in the hand-quilted crosshatching I use throughout the background. It adds texture and dimension to the straight-line quilting and gives uniformity to the piece as a whole.

Linda M. Roy
nnlin2@tds.net
Knoxville, Tennessee

Frame Quilting

When I am quilting a large quilt, I "square it up" before mounting it in a frame, so there's no guesswork that the two sides and top and bottom are equal. I use four boards and C-clamps to make a frame that sits on quilt stands. I never baste a large quilt; I can just as easily quilt lines to stabilize all three layers.

The quilt should be taut, but leave enough "give" so that it will be easier to use the rocking motion with the quilting needle. I often quilt sparsely, leaving the remainder to lap quilt with a hoop. I use clear surgical tape on the finger that is under the quilt. I can feel the needle, but the tape protects my finger.

Kathleen McCrady
kjmccrady@sbcglobal.net
Austin, Texas

Detail, Six x Six, Kathleen McCrady, Austin, Texas

Quilting Landscape Quilts

Country Roads, Nancy Prince, Orlando, Florida.

Nancy Prince
www.nancyprince.com
Orlando, Florida

The quilting detail in landscape quilts should create the illusion that one area is far away, while another is closer. To achieve this, distant areas should have quilting detail close together and, conversely, areas that are closer to the viewer should have quilting detail further apart.

For example, at a horizon where mountains meet the sky, you'd need small, even tiny, stipple detail while the foreground would need topographical detail spaced farther apart. Let the landscape do the talking when determining the quilting detail.

Relief Sculptures

Think of how coins have images that project off of the surface of the metal. I achieve this type of depth in my quilting by stippling very loosely (or not at all) in areas that I want to "come off" the surface and stippling very tightly and small scale in areas that I want to recede.

Combined with the color placement, this sculpturing is particularly effective in portrait quilts. In my quilt MOON DANCE, the viewer has the impression that the face has more depth, due to the very tight stippling around the eyes and nose that creates the relief.

Annette M. Hendricks
www.quiltinglife.com
Grayslake, Illinois

Detail, MOONDANCE, Annette M. Hendricks, Grayslake, Illinois.

Detail, WREATH WITH BIRDS 2006, Julia
Zgliniec, Poway, California

Background square added.

Recreating Quilting

To recreate a quilting pattern, you can use the original quilt to make quilting stencils. Put the quilt on a scanner, scan the quilting patterns, and print them out.

Cover the printed scans with clear contact paper and use an X-Acto® knife to cut out stencil channels. Use the stencil to mark a new quilt for hand or machine quilting.

Julia Zgliniec
rzglini1@san.rr.com
Poway, California

Busy Backs

A tip I pass along to all my students is very simple. Choose a "busy back" for your quilt. When you use something plain, it makes it easier for the judges to see those tiny little errors! The busy backing will mask them all.

Michele Scott
www.piecefulquilter.com
Philadelphia, Pennsylvania

Ursula (aka Glitter Gams), Michele Scott, Philadelphia, Pennsylvania.

Relax!

You will notice that what sets many award-winning quilters apart from the crowd is the fact that they absolutely LOVE to do the work they do.

When you are absolutely in love with what you are creating and the processes that you use to create them, you become relaxed and enter into "the zone" where your work seems to rise to a level beyond what you had imagined possible for yourself to accomplish.

The most important step you can take to relax is choosing to embark only on the projects you really, really adore.

Nichole Webb
kwiltsaq@yahoo.com
Phoenix, Arizona

Background shapes added

Detail, Quilt Lace × Roses × Nichole Webb, Phoenix, Arizona

Love the Mechanics

So many quilters find their enthusiasm and creativity waning by the time they get to the quilting. The quilting stitches are what make the quilt special and the choosing of outline methods, motifs, and backgrounds can be just as creative and exciting as the fun we have choosing fabrics, colors, and designs for the quilt top.

The quilting not only holds the quilt together, but gives it texture, relief, and emphasis where you want it. Whether by hand or machine, domestic or longarm, learn to love the mechanics of the whole process and you will have more finished quilts.

Irene Mueller
sew4th@charter.net
Kirkwood, Missouri

Detail, Fine Dining At Al Fresco, Irene Mueller, Kirkwood, Missouri

Detail, ICE STORM, Suzanne Mouton Riggio, Wauwatosa, Wisconsin.

Be Original

I am inspired by others' art, by nature, and by the world around me. But when the pressure is on, I want to do something I have not seen elsewhere, something that obeys the principles and elements of art that, with the addition of color and texture, will grab the attention of the viewer.

It is of the utmost importance to consider an original, unique design for your own work.

Suzanne Mouton Riggio
quzanne@aol.com
Wauwatosa, Wisconsin

Passion

Finishing Touches

To Border or Not?

There are several reasons to add borders to quilts: to make them larger, to frame the quilt, to use all the fabric you bought for the project, etc. Borders are much more interesting if they become part of the quilt design.

Take some extra time to preview border designs. This can be done by cutting and sewing a few pieces or by drafting some ideas with pencil and graph paper.

Alice Arnett
www.alicekayquilts.com
Laramie, Wyoming

Detail, ORIENTAL SPIRAL, Alice Kay Arnett, Laramie, Wyoming.

Borders

While it is quick and easy to stitch on a length of fabric, I consider a pieced border the ultimate in border-dom. A busy interior can be calmed or a quiet quilt body can be jazzed up. Design elements from within the quilt can be carried out into the frame, either precisely or subtly. Curves can counter sharp points and straight lines. Random piecing in the border makes a great foil for rigid construction in the blocks.

It is amazing how much a border can add, and a pieced border can be the real frosting on the cake.

Jane Hall
www.janehallquilts.com
Raleigh, North Carolina

INDIGO LIGHTS, Jane Hall, Raleigh, North Carolina.

Piping

Piping adds a distinctive flair and professional finish to a quilt's binding, but can be tricky to do well. Choose 1/16" or 1 mm. cording with a smooth finish. It will make perfect, tiny piping and won't cause lumpy corners the way thicker cording will.

Cut bias strips, join them, press in half lengthwise, wrong sides together, and tuck the cording into the fold. Place a stack of 10 Post-it® notes to the left of the machine needle and next to the fold, to keep the piping from wandering away while you stitch close to the cording.

Finally, use my Groovin' Piping Trimming Tool to trim the seam allowance to a consistent width.

Susan K. Cleveland
www.piecesbewithyou.com.
West Concord, Minnesota

Detail, Bouncin', Susan K. Cleveland, West Concord, Minnesota

Launder First

Nearly all newly finished quilts look better after laundering. Any accumulated soil is removed; the batting puffs up between the lines of the stitching, highlighting the quilting; and the fabric puckers up around the lines of stitching, camouflaging any minor irregularities.

I launder before binding so I can block and square the quilt. I zigzag stitch the quilt edges and clip the corners on the backing fabric before washing in cold water, on gentle cycle, with Orvus® quilt soap. I lay the quilt out as flat and square as I can get it and let it dry completely without disturbing it. Finally, I square up the quilt by trimming away excess batting and backing, then apply the binding.

Scott Murkin
www.scottmurkin.com
Asheboro, North Carolina

Hybrid, Scott Murkin, Asheboro, North Carolina. Insert: detail.

Sleeving

I always put a sleeve at the bottom of any of my quilts that are not miniatures. The bottom sleeve is smaller than the top one. I use the same size stick in that as I do at the top of the quilt. This helps the quilt hang better.

Before I add the binding, I measure all four sides of the quilt, cut ¼" twill tape to those measurements, and stitch the tape to the edges of the quilt. It is hidden by the binding and gives the quilt a firm edge so that it will hang straight.

Janet Steadman
http://www2.Whidbey.net/jandon/Pages/Galleries.html
Langley, Washington

A Fine Romance, Janet Steadman, Langley, Washington.

Detail, Birds of Paradise, Karolyn Reker, Cartersville, Georgia.

No Fold Lines

I have tried several ways of folding quilts to be mailed to quilt shows. I have been very disappointed to see a crease still showing after a quilt has been hanging.

An article by Ann Fahl in *Quilters Newsletter* recommended folding quilts on the bias to eliminate fold marks. I tried it and it works! Quilts that have been sitting in tight boxes and quilts I have to fold to store at home don't get creases. Just keep doing folds on the diagonal until the quilt is the size you want for storing or shipping.

Karolyn Reker
karolynskuilts@yahoo.com
Cartersville, Georgia

Document Your Quilts

I keep an index card file for every quilt I make. I record the title, when it was made, how long it took, fabric costs, size, who it was made for or who bought it and for how much, why it was made (show, commission, challenge, etc.), who quilted it, type of batting used, where it was shown or published, appraised value, and what awards it won.

I also keep a photo record, but in a separate album as well as on the computer. By doing this, I can track down the quilts for exhibitions, be sure I don't show the same quilt in the same place twice, and have all the information ready if I need it for a publication.

Anne Morrell Robinson
www.kingrossquilts.com
Margaree Valley, Nova Scotia, Canada

Ode to Cotton and Indigo, Anne Morrell Robinson, Margaree Valley, Nova Scotia, Canada. Inset detail.

Background square added.

Good Photos

Document your work with photos that are sharp and clear, with accurate color representation, taken on a neutral background, with no fingers, toes, or cats in the picture. Great photographs are essential for entries to juried exhibitions, Web sites and blogs, press releases, business cards, and stationery.

Use professional photographers, insisting on something called "work for hire," which means you retain the photo copyright. Credit the photographer wherever and whenever you use the photos. If you should lose or damage a quilt, sell it, or give it away, you will always have a record of your work.

Kim Ritter
www.kimritter.com
Houston, Texas

Doing the Can-Can, Kim Ritter, Houston, Texas. Inset: quilt detail. Background rectangle added.

Be One of a Kind

Create what you love with every fiber of your being. Don't construct quilts to win awards or to follow trends. Be brave and bold. If you like small quilts, make small quilts. If you

Detail, NAPOLEON, Michael Aaron McAllister, St. Louis, Missouri.

like crazy quilts, make the craziest one out there! Bead them, embroider them, beribbon them. Do what brings you optimum joy.

At the end of the day, you are the only person you need to please. It's better to be a first-rate original than a second-rate imitation.

Passion

Michael Aaron McAllister
www.michaelaaronmcallister.com
St. Louis, Missouri

Detail, JAPANESE GARDEN, Clairan Ferrono, Chicago, Illinois.

Keep It All Straight

If you're planning to enter a show, remember to keep your dates straight. Make sure you know if the due date for quilt images is a "postmarked by" or a "received by" date.

If it's "received by," be sure to mail your slides or CD in plenty of time. It's not unusual for mail to take longer than you expect for it to arrive. Be on the safe side and mail your entry early.

Clairan Ferrono
www.fabric8tions.net
Chicago, Illinois

Entry Photographs

Most shows require a full and detailed picture of your finished quilt. Your quilt should be the only object in the photograph. Keep these four factors in mind:

- Frame — Use a single lens reflex (SLR) camera. Get as close to the margins as you can without cropping.
- Clarity — Use a tripod for crisp details.
- Even lighting — Sunshine causes shadows, so shoot outside on a cloudy day or inside against a gray sheet pinned to your design wall. Do not use a flash.
- Color — Use an exposure disc set to set the white balance to whatever light you are shooting in. Your colors will read correctly.

Kathy McNeil
www.kathymcneilquilts.com
Marysville, Washington

Detail, Tudor Romance, Kathy McNeil, Marysville, Washington.

Submitting Your Photographs

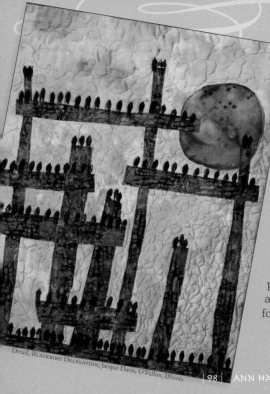

Detail, BLACKBIRD DELEGATION, Jacque Davis, O'Fallon, Illinois.

Understand the entry requirements before pictures are taken because they are not the same for every show. The primary methods for submitting photographs are e-mail (jpeg format is most common) or postal mail with a CD, floppy disc, or photographic slide. Whatever method you use, be sure to include the name and quilt information required by the show.

Most shows require a full view and a detail shot. Remove any lint or loose threads. Hire a professional if you can. Your photo must not be altered. Remember to kiss your entry goodbye for good luck!

Jacque Davis
davis4andmike@yahoo.com
O'Fallon, Illinois

Fused Art Quilts

If your quilt is fused, do not let anyone handle the quilt. They sometimes can't resist trying to pick at the quilt and sometimes will pull the fabric right off.

Keep fused quilts out of direct light. Do not fold a fused quilt. Roll it on a tube or keep it flat instead.

Laura Wasilowski
www.laurawasilowski.com
Elgin, Illinois

Yellow Chair Loves Apples, Laura Wasilowski, Elgin, Illinois.

Detail, Peacock, Dixie McBride, Eureka, California. Center of quilt shown.

Catch the Judge's Eye

In traditional quilts, you need a shining example of the category. All techniques should be handled well, including an effective use of color and hanging straight.

In innovative quilts, you need all of the above including attention-grabbing choice of colors, a different way of putting your blocks together, and a certain degree of difficulty.

Art quilts have to be original, unique in design elements and composition. Anything less is considered an adaptation.

You want your quilt to stand out and make the judges stop and say, "Wow!," whatever the category.

Dixie McBride
www.dixiemcbride.com
Eureka, California

Judging

It is helpful to understand why you are entering a show. Most quilters enter a show because they want to share their work or earn an award and recognition. But judging is based on different things.

Accuracy, ability, and interpretation are among the things judges look for. But you might be making a statement or have a goal that one particular judge just doesn't see. Enter the quilt in another show and you'll see a completely different set of remarks.

I look forward to seeing if the judges' comments match my own thoughts. Don't make a quilt just for the judges. Let your own personality come out and make it for yourself first!

A WALK IN THE WOODS, Katherine Alyce, Plainfield, Vermont. Background rectangle added.

Katherine Alyce
www.waterfallquilts.com
Plainfield, Vermont

Send Thank-You Notes

Detail, YOU ARE IN, Judy Rush, Bexley, Ohio.

Always send thank-you notes! If you receive an award, sell your work, or are invited to participate in an event, send a thank-you to the people who supplied the award or the organization that supported the event. It is a kind and generous thing to do for the people who have made the effort to supply the award, and they will remember the correspondence.

Everyone likes to get USPS mail. Personalize the thank-you with an image of the award-winning work. You can make some pretty amazing cards these days and the extra effort will be appreciated!

Judy Rush
www.judyrush.com
Bexley, Ohio

Have a Play Day

Passion

I set aside a couple of days now and then to make a series of tiny collages. Start with a 5" x 7" area. Simply cut out shapes in a spontaneous way and play with the design and color.

This never fails to get ideas flowing to launch a new project. Arrange a "play day" with a group of quilting pals with the aim of sharing new techniques and working on a small quick projects like artist's trading cards or postcards. It is very inspirational!

Valerie Hearder
www.valeriehearder.com
Nova Scotia, Canada

Detail, LIFE LINE: DISPLACEMENT, Valerie Hearder, Nova Scotia, Canada.

Detail, Pont en Royans, Lenore Crawford, Midland, Michigan.

Passion

Be inspired to create art that you love, not art that is dictated by what someone else thinks you should do. Keep learning new techniques to make your art more interesting and to keep from getting stagnant.

Change helps keep my art fresh by adding new techniques to my style, which continues to evolve.

Lenore Crawford
www.lenorecrawford.com
Midland, Michigan